THIS IS ABOUT INCEST

THIS
IS ABOUT
INCEST

by
Margaret
Randall

Firebrand
Books
Ithaca, New York

This book may not be reproduced in whole or in part, except in the case of reviews, without permission from Firebrand Books, Ithaca, New York 14850.

Book design by Mary A. Scott
Cover design by Betsy Bayley
Typesetting by Bets Ltd.

Printed on acid-free paper in the United States by McNaughton & Gunn.

This publication is made possible, in part, with support from the Literature Panel, New York State Council on the Arts.

Library of Congress Cataloging-in-Publication Data

Randall, Margaret, 1936–
    This is about incest.

    1. Incest—United States. 2. Randall, Margaret,
1936–   . 3. Incest victims—United States—
Biography. I. Title.
HQ72.U53R35 1987   306.7'77   87–412
ISBN 0–932379–30–3 (alk. paper)
ISBN 0–932379–29–X (pbk. : alk. paper)

This book is for Becky Bosch
who helped retrieve the memory,
for my parents
who (knowingly and unknowingly)
provided a buffer of love,
and for my sisters and brothers
working to survive.

Contents

If the following prose, poems, and photographic images are taken in the order in which they are offered, the reader/viewer will have the chronological journey as close as possible to that which I experienced and wish to share.

The Story

Each of us is here now because in one way or another we share a commitment to language and to the power of language, and to the reclaiming of that language which has been made to work against us. In the transformation of silence into language and action, it is vitally necessary for each of us to establish or examine her function in that transformation and to recognize her role as vital within that transformation.

Audre Lorde*

1. This is about the language.

I want you to know that for me a poem or piece of short prose has a life not fully understood by most people. My work changes from its moment of conception. It grows, and doesn't stop when—considered "finished"—it occupies a clean sheet of paper, presents itself in impeccable arrangement on the page, or begins its travels in envelopes to be shared with friends, to magazine and book editors, or to auditoriums where it will be heard in oral form.

More than any other event, repeated oral sharings can change my poems. Words get added, left out, moved around. Often there is the sudden realization that a finished work ends several lines before it at first appeared to. Its added verbiage was simply the winding down, an inability to move away from a completed idea, a failure to recognize the end. A rush when hearing the words in certain circumstances, the electricity in a room, or the silent response from the eyes of a single person in the audience can change a poem completely.

*"The Transformation of Silence into Language and Action," collected in *Sister Outsider* by Audre Lorde (Crossing Press, 1984).

And memory plays its part here. How do we forget for so long? How do we suddenly remember? What juxtaposition of words, what silent signal, what contact of eyes, what veil abruptly lifted, brings back knowledge, prods our lips to speak?

A good poem doesn't describe an event. It *becomes* the experience for each of us in as many ways as there are readers or listeners bringing our own memory and need to bear upon what has happened.

When what is shared is incest, there is another dimension. Incest has been experienced by so many of us but has been cast from our memory banks or pushed into their most inaccessible corners by a socialization that has told us, "No...go away... you are not real... you are not a part of *me!*" We are expertly taught. All that matters is the surface. Keep up appearances. Fit in. Don't rock the boat. Never wash your dirty laundry in public. Keep the peace.

Writing about incest is at once necessary (exploration, exorcism?) and painful for the writer. It is also often tenuous—the source itself floating somewhere just beyond consciousness. For the listener or reader it is uncomfortable, perhaps demanding, especially if the revived experience taps into something of her own, until now safely stored, adroitly camouflaged.

There is a need for a great literalness. Step by step. Here, I will take you by the hand....

2. This is about the small me.

I was the oldest in a middle-class, white, urban-to-suburban family of two daughters and a son. Our home had books, art, travel, a dog. As I look back over close to fifty years of my life, and what I know of the lives of my mother and father, the greatest obstacle to clear self-knowledge that I am now able to identify is the fact that my parents were not impelled—either by society or themselves—to question in any depth their own particular deprivation and pain.

I grew up in a home where there was love. There was comfort, and adventure. My parents respected my brother, sister, and myself, and did as much as they could to allow us to explore our needs and choose our options—even when they did not understand or like them. They taught us honesty, a love for others, curiosity. And they tried to defend us against those who wronged us.

My grandparents were somehow "other," although they variously did everything possible to be acceptable within their visions of the society they lived to emulate. For my father's parents, money spoke louder than any other commodity. For my mother's parents it was good taste, refinement, "the proper way to act" which assured, in turn, the proper way to be.

On my father's side my grandfather died before I was born. I knew him only in pictures: German immigrant, self-made man, reserved from his three sons, more given to speaking with money than with an embrace. Emotion was not something he showed. My father's mother was beautiful, pampered, ignorantly simple, generous in ways that pleased her, a somewhat superficial woman who kept a Jewish home and had an Irish maid.

On my mother's side there were more extremes. My grand-mother was a rancorously self-indulgent woman who emptied ashtrays while her guests were smoking and rearranged sofa cushions the minute her guests rose to their feet. She had a special and constant way of making you feel you had slighted or annoyed her. She was the classic martyr figure.

My maternal grandfather is the hidden protagonist of this un-folding. The man who raped me, hiding his abuse in my tender years, in my inability to define, fight back, or reveal. As a child and young woman I knew him as the travelling jewelry sales-man turned dreamy Christian Science practitioner, the strange healer, the quiet gentleman who would take me to a museum or the Oyster Bar at Grand Central Station. Later, in the New York of my young adulthood, he was the patriarch who disap-proved of my lifestyle and friends.

At times my parents found their parents uncomfortable. Difficult to be around. Tolerable. . . but barely. Eventually my mother and father moved their own family west, among other things to put some distance between our lives and their origins. In the conflicts that arose between my mother's family and me—the later conflicts, the known conflicts, the ones that were a part of my few years as a would-be writer and single mother in New York—my parents usually took my side, defending my right to be as I was against my maternal grandparents' freely offered criticism.

I have moved back and forth in my need—no, not in my need but in my ability—to talk with my mother about the incest is-sue. She has wanted to be supportive, and has been, far beyond what many mothers would have mustered. It is clearly painful for her as well. One day we can speak; the next her concern for a dead father—the aggressor—shuts my doors again. It has been beautiful to have the opportunity of seeing her legitimate love, she who so rarely expresses unedited feelings. Then, after a conversation particularly moving to me, she gets a migraine. And I retreat once more.

3. This is about the mushrooms.

As a child I hated summer camp for a single terrifying reason: more likely than not, there would be mushrooms growing in the woods surrounding the campsite. Once I remember hiding for hours when my campmates, after marvelling at the different varieties, collected and brought back to our tent a number of awful specimens. In fifth grade I suffered an incident that would haunt me for years. Straying from the rest of my class during a school picnic, I could not make myself rejoin them when I noticed a large toadstool between where I had strayed and the group. Other events, events I feared and was somehow always waiting for, threatened to reveal my terrible secret until I managed, with increasing skill, to avoid confronting the phobia. I learned how to give a wide berth to that part of the supermarket, beg off when picnics were planned, sense what I might find pictured in a book before I came to the offending page.

All my conscious life I have feared mushrooms—their sight, their smell, the possibility of their presence, something to be found in unexpected places and that grow so quickly, almost while one watches. The terrifying thought was that I might come into actual physical contact with them. Worse, one might somehow enter me. Even now my body orifices close almost automatically at the thought (threat).

There is no known memory before this fear. It goes back to my earliest childhood, and has accompanied me through the most agonizing as well as the cleverest of subterfuges and justifications. This is fear beyond fear, called phobia by the makers of psychological language.

Even the word *phobia* seems inadequate; for xenophobia (the fear of foreigners) and homophobia (the fear of homosexuality) are prejudices susceptible to education. When people I've known have described agoraphobia (the fear of being in the midst of open spaces), or claustrophobia (the fear of being closed in), I have imagined a likeness, in intensity, to my fear of mushrooms. But only a likeness. Like all those who suffer the effects of phobias, I believe no one can truly understand the consuming horror of mine.

Throughout my life, sporadically, I've tried different methods I thought might ease or release the fear. People insisted, "Well, I'm sure if you just confronted the fear. . ." (like "if you really wanted to stop smoking, you would" or "if you really wanted to be thin, you'd just eat less. . .is that really so difficult?"). This is one of the many negative legacies imposed upon us by our Judeo-Christian formation. A friend who was also a psychologist once tried hypnosis, but with too little time for any really useful exploration. A psychiatrist, perhaps faced with his own ineptness at even touching the origins, told me I should be happy to have such a single strong fear. "And of something you can simply avoid," he added. This man, to whom I paid $35 an hour in the mid-1950s, tried to make me believe that "having all your fears in one basket" has its advantages!

In Nicaragua, a psychologist named Tony helped me to make the decision to return to the United States and assured me I would be able to work through the fear. In Albuquerque, Becky is the therapist—and dear friend—who has helped me break through the invisible membrane, identify incest as its source, and continue this necessary journey home.

4. I am a woman.

Feminism was essential. First to the gradual self-knowledge of my own worth, as a woman and as women. Then to the slow repossession of my strength. Then to the realization that my fear is rooted in a part of my woman's history denied in order that I function in the world as it is. And finally to my certainty that I would be able to work through the memory, the terror, the ghosts, the meaning, and damage to a more useful regrouping of self.

Patriarchy denies the worth of women. The worth of children. Except as sustainers, objects of maintenance and pleasure. We are servants guaranteeing reproduction, production's bottom line. Capitalism stratifies the denial; advanced capitalism streamlines it. The girl child is denied by gender and by age. Class and race often conspire to deepen the oppression.

But incest seems ignorant of class, race, or social status. Recent studies show that 80 percent of children are victimized by an adult they know and trust. And it is overwhelmingly a male crime. In one serious study of incestuous abuse cases, 97 percent of the offenders were adult males and 87 percent of the child victims were females.[1]

"As long as we continue a structure of family life based on a unit headed by a patriarchal figure, however benevolent, we may be endangering the lives of the women and children in that unit. Feminist theory reminds us that even as we deal with individual acts of sexual and physical violence committed by men, it is the power concentrated in the hands of one gender that is the fundamental social problem."[2]

The female child, double commodity in a consumer society, suffers her greatest invisibility at the hands of the male authority figure abusing her in incest.

The reclamation of worth, with its accompanying reclamation of rights, must, in fact, include a reclamation of memory.

5. This is about discovery. Unfolding.

Incest. My grandfather. The Christian Science practitioner. The man from whom I recoiled and toward whom I felt vaguely guilty because I never understood why he evoked such seemingly inappropriate feelings in me. My grandfather. The man who abused me when I was too young to fight back. Or when my only way of fighting back was to obliterate the event, transfer the event into another, greater fear.

I am sure I bring to therapy a series of signs, a complex of internal battles that—seen and felt by a skilled and caring counselor, and in the light of so much recently revealed experience—provokes the right questions, a door that opens. There is bodywork, and there are connections. Words that unlock at precisely the right moments opening new doors. Without a women's movement, without developments in feminist theory, this could not have been possible—for me, or for thousands.

The day this knowledge surfaced in my body and my mind, all the complex questions were secondary. There was no doubt. Rarely have I been so sure of anything.

True to my conditioning, there is a disjuncture between my mind and body in their separate ways of touching my history. I have always been good at working things out with my head. Indeed, my fine and dependable head seems to have made the incest bearable precisely by making the intellectual transference from unacceptable (unavoidable) abuse to neat (pocketed) horror.

Now I am teaching my body to go back, to identify the act, to work through the terror and anger—replacing them where I could not focus as an infant—and to understand how the abuse informed other areas of my action and reaction as well.

How does one sit on a floor in a room, confront the fear, retrieve the memory? How does one arrange old pictures, feel the chest constrict, push the hand toward the feared object, touch it move it place it right there where it must be dealt with in his lap or just by his mouth, touch it touch it feel the pain deep within the left eye, breathe. . . that's it . . . breathe deeply, touch, recoil, allow the feelings in. And out. What do you want to say? What do you want to tell him?

The camera is ready, take it in your hand, focus and see, focus first on his face, on you as a tiny child, on the mushroom, focus focus. . . . Why is the focus so hard to hold? I get his eyes, clear as their purpose. Or I get my own small features. His. Mine. His. Mine. Mine. . .and the mushroom, moving back and forth between the two. And I focus again, and I shoot, focus and shoot, bringing it up. And out.

My mouth tastes funny now. I want to vomit. Saliva flows and flows, my mouth is filling with it, overflowing with it. Am I drooling? Filling, filling . . . and then I know. I know what he made me do. I know what he did to me. Another piece in the puzzle. Another memory retrieved.

How do you do this, in one hour, unfold then fold again . . . at least long enough to survive, at least until the next time? And the next. How do you do this work after the post office and before class, after breakfast with a friend and before the shopping list, after protection, before the poem? You do it with help. You do it with a sister. You do it with a sensitive caring professional. You do it with your self-knowledge, you as woman, as survivor. Coming whole. You do it like this.

6. This is about memory.

Having come back to the United States after twenty-three years in Latin America, returning to New Mexico, the land of my growing up, after such participatory years in Mexico, Cuba, Nicaragua, I found reentry exciting—and fragmenting.

High tech, intense specialization, and the daily effect of the media all seem to conspire to keep the parts of my being in perpetual separateness. I wanted to pull together the varied strands of my roots in this country and my experiences in Latin America; I wanted to find my center, and my whole.

A struggle with the U.S. Immigration and Naturalization Service to be able to remain here in some ways intensified the fragmentation: the political battle fortified my center, while the daily grappling with a capitalist bureaucracy's version of human rights constantly jarred and shifted my sense of self.

In the midst of this many-layered reentry process, the "memory" of incest broke to the surface, demanded I address it.

I use the word *memory* with reservations, but also with intent. I can feel, oh so deeply, the memory of my grandfather's abuse, but am only just beginning to be able to articulate its substance, its detail. Sound, but no words. Recognition in the body without always the precision of total descriptive power.

Memory can prove deception as well as tool. In my last difficult days of Nicaraguan death, my memory crashed, its pieces colliding with each other and with me. I would forget a conversation that had taken place only a day or two before. A street might suddenly emerge with a piece of eighteenth-century history sitting on its shoulder. "White spots" was a literal description of how my mind would empty for a fraction of a second during a reading or lecture.

An oppressive system's most finely honed weapon against a people's self-knowledge is the expert distortion of that people's collective memory. And so Vietnam becomes a page of glory, Three Mile Island a nonevent, and Chernobyl the first devastating nuclear accident in history. McCarthyism a denial alive even today. A constant media hype decides for us what we like and dislike, what we trust and don't, if and with whom and how we must pair, how many children we should have, what kind of education we have a right to expect, what kind of job we will hold, where and how we will live, what we will wear. And how originally we may think, and what. We are trained to see others as "other," different; we are programmed to forget how alike we are. And so they keep us divided.

Now we know that the women analyzed by Freud were not fantasizing, but speaking out of painful memory of their abuse suffered at the hands of fathers, uncles, friends of the family.

And we know that Freud knew this, his own formation and prejudice (privilege) keeping him from announcing the revelation that would have helped free us long ago. His theory of "the hysterical woman." His theory of woman's fantasy.

But, of course, *we* must free *ourselves*.

Under patriarchy, in a commodity-oriented society, continuity is removed from history so that human movement falls into step in one giant game of follow the leader.

When memory stood as the key to my absence and presence in this world, I looked at the ways in which our collective memory is manipulated—at times mutilated—in order that we forget who we are, what we have done, our feelings. And our strengths.

And I inserted within this general sense of memory/non-memory the incest experience. How Freud prevented generations of women from making contact with our memories, substituting the idea of fantasy for our history of abuse. How in my own case I had "forgotten" my grandfather's incestuous assault, replacing it with the phobia—a fear that blotted out the fearful.

When I first understood this transference, I saw it only as the obliteration of real memory, the development of an alternate memory which kept me from making the necessary connections. Then I saw it another way. The phobia became the safeguard of my memory, the place where it could be stored, the memory bank from which I would someday be able to retrieve it, retrieve and deal with it. That someday is now.

I do not think the second explanation negates the first. In some as yet unexplained way, they are complementary.

7. This is about being an artist.

Almost without realizing what I was doing, I began to use my particular creativity to explore the incest of which (some would say) I was victim, from which (some would say) I survived. (At this point on my journey, I would say we are much more than victims. Survivors, yes, but always damaged, always scarred, most often with wounds forever raw.)

The process pushed me to write—first poetry, then prose. Soon there was a sheaf of poems. My skills as an oral historian came to the fore in the search for old pictures, old letters . . .a particular use of this material. And as a photographer I went into the darkroom. Each time an image came up in the developer, I relived, and worked with, a piece of the abuse I was learning to confront.

The therapy became a place where I felt safe enough to push forward, and confident that I could. Becky's skill and sensitivity gave me growth. "I guess I should put the mushroom back in the bag," I said at the end of a session one day, and reached out. "If you think you *should*, I'll do it for you," she said, and quickly did just that. The pressure is there to become whole. So is the message that there is time, time to do it at my own pace.

And Becky has welcomed my need to photograph this retrieval, or start a session by reading a poem in which my memory reconstructs the damage. . .and the hope.

I find it profoundly moving and satisfying to know that I am working at this task—a task which will no doubt occupy me, in one way or another, for as long as I live—within the context of my art.

8. This is about the old poems, the unconscious ones.

When in his ninetieth year my grandfather died, my mother travelled from New Mexico to New York to be with him through his last days in the hospital. For some reason I remember the phrase "she went to give blood," as if the main sense of it was a gift—meaningless, too late—that she could give, as well as her presence beside his bed. When she returned she spoke of his refusal to be comforted by the reading of his holy book, *Science and Health With Key to the Scriptures*. He waved it away with a weak hand, and somehow indicated that then, in his moment of truth, he no longer believed. This was spoken of at some length. It seemed sad that upon his deathbed he could not have "the comfort he had given others."

Sometime during my mother's absence, sometime before the news of my grandfather's death actually reached me, I wrote the following poem:[3]

The Dying Grandfather Where There Was No Love

I don't know if he's dead yet.
Maybe he died a few days ago, the mail
takes so long, I don't know.

He almost died Wednesday morning my father said
and then rallied, then
went out again
but not completely. Hearing my father's voice

saying mother went 2,000 miles
to give a dying man blood, her father.
The useless wait, the useless words, consoling,
maybe even real.

I don't deny the possibility.
I don't deny the probability, somewhere, perhaps
someone must care, perhaps
his wife. After all.

I only wonder that my own emotion
is nowhere past the curious
question
and answer. That far apart.
That dead.

"My own emotion . . . nowhere." Nowhere, at least, where I could find it then. A curious poem. But not so curious now that I know more. Now that circumstance and meaning are beginning to come clear in me.

Some years later I put together a small book called *We*, a collection of nine prose portraits of people who had been important in my life.[4] Each of these men or women had made an impact in a positive way. I admired or loved them. Each, that is, except my grandfather. My grandfather was included in this collection, the only portrait evoking what I thought to be an indifferent or negative personality. Perhaps I believed that one had to love one's grandfather and wondered at the seemingly undefined emotions surrounding mine. I had always thought love the unifying thread in this collection. Now I see it as impact—impact upon a life, my own, impact both positive (in eight of the portraits) and devastating (in one). The portrait is called "In A Plastic Bag":

Quiet and stately. White, almost-powdered face. Unperturbed except on your deathbed when you didn't want to die. Then it all seemed to fall apart. The half-century memories of Yellowstone National Park. Nana Jo, her pursed lips and her enema bag, her exemplary puffed cushions and spotless ashtrays, her Eleanor Roosevelt and potted plants. The healing power of mind over matter, the refrigerator full of *beah* instead of the forbidden *beer*, the women who came to you in tears, the healing power of Mary Baker Eddy and the cases where "the doctors gave up" and you took over. The collection of socks: ninety-seven complete pairs, twenty-one used, seventy-six new, four odd singles (used). The collection of cameras. All from Abercrombie & Fitch ads. The times you took me—little girl in a navy blue coat with white peter pan collar—to the Oyster Bar at Grand Central, or to open your office safe and look at the cut and polished stones. All seeming to fall apart, to fall apart, and the sentences finally couldn't complete themselves and then there were no more sentences and the nonendings ended and your daughter—my own mother—said they came to get you, took your pajamas off, packaged you in a plastic bag and took you away.

In my still-numbed state, it was my vision of you that fell apart. Today, with so much more knowledge, I would write this piece quite differently.

I read it, and suddenly put reason to the fact that only now, nearing fifty, have I begun to enjoy having potted plants in the house. My desire to nurture them, watch them grow, has exactly paralled my work with the incest.

9. The words and images of today.

What follows, in nearly chronological order, are the words and images of today. Poems from a process of unfolding, from a process of hard work—confrontation and discovery. Images from long ago, pictures taken from a family album, reclaiming a lost dimension. A task only just begun, which does not pretend to be more than it is: the markings of an ongoing journey. Unique and collective. Images and words speaking a language we must take the power to change.

Notes

1. *Conspiracy of Silence: The Trauma of Incest* by Sandra Butler (Volcano Press, San Francisco, 1985), pp. 5-6.

2. Ibid., p. 212

3. *Part of the Solution* by Margaret Randall (New Directions Publishers, New York, 1972).

4. *We* by Margaret Randall (Smyrna Press, New York, 1978).

The Poems

Killing The Saint

Your father   My grandfather   The Saint
The parts of his body
are taking back their names.
Once you say yes,
maybe he also forced my brother.
Maybe he forced me.

But now again you don't remember.
I didn't say that, you tell me, tonight.
I never said that.
Flashes of mirror
pinning wet clothes
to a line in moonlight. Fear.

Mother you are larger now.
Awkward, we split.
The mirror goes.

A year passes and another, we don't
talk about these things (we
who are called close)
we don't say these things
without a neat period, sufficient commas.

Then one day I use the hard-won memory
sit before you, and begin.
You say the right thing, it has
taken me years
to understand your answers
are often that: words
speaking to themselves.
Words moving in unison
put a good face forward. Everyone claps.

Mother when your demons loom
and you become larger than life
my children grow small
on that horizon.
As you pull
I lose them one by one.
Or is it me I lose?
Or is it me I fear
to lose?

In this poem I hold your eyes
and shout
please mother don't say the words
you think we want.
Speak from your own fear.

Look, I am bringing my children back, circling
their size.

Killing The Saint
in his thirty years of death.

Touching the rotten flesh
in moonlight. Watching the pillars fall.
Retrieving their pieces.

Enter The White-Faced Man

Against the learned response, a word, any word at all
my body says retreat.
Again and again the man in the perfect three-piece suit
enters.
Enter the white-faced man.

(The entering. I am
broken,
bought and spent.)

Is this my aversion to business suits, their vests, their ties?
And when did my memory veer off course,
when I left?
when you left?
when you died?

I don't want your hands
on this half-century of film.
I don't want your business suit,
flat white face too close to mine.
Your rimless glasses
get in my way.

Whoever said the peaceful dead?

I need to kill you *my* way.
You, more alive than you were
the day we said our mute good-byes.

Learning To Remember

Waiting too long
to set the image down
is another way of saying no.
I don't want to look at you now.

It goes meekly then, among easier tasks.
Cries where no one hears.
Fades into memory
acceptably imperfect.

Can I trust this trembling,
accept these hands whitened
not by death but by a new light
shining from my core?

Learning to listen
to the body closing
to the image asking
to be taken seriously, loved.

Learning to remember,
learning against all odds
to break your chain in me.

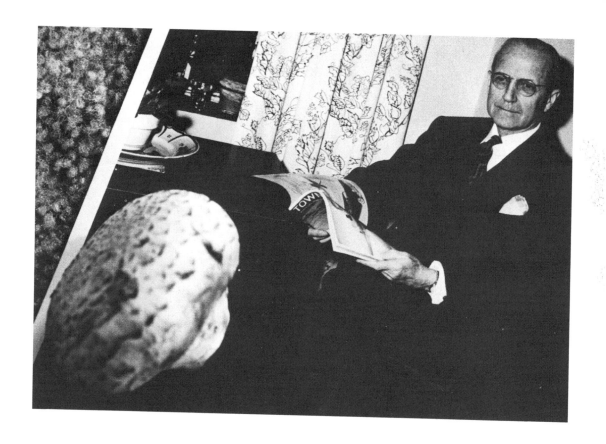

Watching It Grow Between Your Legs

Grandpa you sit in formal portraiture,
image of your transatlantic mal de mer
that is also timeless,
no date to help me through,
no known piercing of history, yours or mine,
except in the way a photo
always stops a life: relentlessly.

Like a dog I sniff your low-key pinstripe suit,
finding scent and order, order and scent,
you sit by a table, legs crossed
pages of a magazine parted across your lap.
The New Yorker
or *Field and Stream* . . .
Abercrombie & Fitch, addiction of your class.

In this portrait nothing betrays your dozens of cameras,
hundreds of unworn socks,
obsession of screwdrivers and pliers.
Nothing beyond your Christian Science eyes,
posture of confirmed authority.
Grandpa there is nothing in this picture
to give you away.

Nobody raises her hand here, nothing but fear.
Oh you were never a healer in me.
The table reflection of patterned drapes
to the only surface
absent of person or place:
your camouflaged whiteness, my torn memory.

Stiffening, closing, I move my hand
until (almost a knowledge
in and of itself)
it picks up the feared piece in this puzzle
and sets it in your lap.
Watching it grow between your legs
I don't need questions.

Still trying to hold without touching,
plugging my memory
into your whitened wall of time,
moving the evidence,
clicking the shutter,
I focus and shoot, focus and shoot,
stalking your picture and its hideous sprout.

These are the things we will never do together,
you who have hidden so long
in death,
I who wrench you from my flesh
breathing or not.
No words. Pure sound.
Pain flooding my left eye.

The Second Photograph

I have found another portrait.
You have me on your lap
flanked by my two grandmothers
both looking congenitally worried
as well they should.
You, on the other hand, seem vaguely crazed
as you certainly were, your lips and eyes
focused on different planes.

I have looked long and hard
at the hands in this picture.
Both women hide theirs, differently.
Yours, Grandpa, are loosely circled
about my three-year-old body.
Your right covers my left, your left
comes round my party-dressed buttocks,
your fingers strangely held, as if in secret sign.

I am reading this into the image.
I am reading it because I know.
I am telling it because now, half a century later,
I understand
why my eyes in the picture
take the camera head on,
demanding answers.

The Letter

I have found a letter dated March 11th, 1959.
"Meg is still our flesh and blood,"
you write your daughter, my mother,
but "conformity to custom in dress and appearance
is wise in every age. . .
it never pays to stand out as a sore thumb in the world."
I live in a building you consider unsafe.
You object to my ponytail, leotards, mascara.
My "extreme radicalism" is bound to harm me.
"In addition," you write, "Meg told us
she poses in the nude."
I have heard that again
more recently.
It was in a deportation hearing.
I was the defendant.

But the line that pulls me back
in this yellowed letter
is where you say,
"It seems that with each crisis in Meg's experience
there had to be someone else to cohabit with.
This seems to be a bit too abnormal."
I wonder why.
I wonder why you found it a bit too abnormal, Grandpa,
when it was you who abused me
before I could speak.
It was you who used my tender baby flesh and mind,
hid behind your patriarch privilege
and left me to figure it out,
left me to wonder who abused you,
and how to clean the fear.

Someone Trusted Has Used Force

The triangle veered
and fell.

From mother/father/child
to home/world/memory. . .
that's me.

Suddenly there are
infinite triangles:
Protect/evade/love,
Force/fear/shut down,
Mind/body/sex,
Lie/be safe/survive. . .

Look/lie/remember,
Retreat/forget/forget,
Comfort/close/fear,
Power/options/hope. . .

Earth/memory/sky,
Water/sky/memory,
Memory/earth/water. . .

Until there is fire
pushing earth and water apart,
sky searing the hands.

Sky burns
and the triangle
no longer holds the child
within familiar sides.

Someone trusted has used force
to enter this space.

Memory tears and shreds.
Life and memory
have both been sacrificed.

Nothing is as it was.

The Green Clothes Hamper

Rain almost hides my mountains today.
Low clouds snag the rocky skirts, colors
of rain and clouds
clean everything.

I speak of the rain, the clouds, the living
colors of this land
because it seems impossible
to cut this silence with the words

my grandfather was a sick and evil man
posing as healer.
Now I retrieve his hands and eyes, his penis
filling my tiny infant mouth

as he forced himself into a body, mine,
that still finds reason easier than feeling.
This is the green lucite top
of a clothes hamper where rape impaled diapers.

This is memory catching up with itself,
overtaking asthma, compulsive food, fear
of that which is not itself.
This lost green hamper. My body coming home.

Let Us Move On

. . .The poet who knows that beautiful language can lie, that the oppressor's language sometimes sounds beautiful.

Adrienne Rich*

Having found the event
I looked for the man.
Having discovered the man
I needed the meaning.

It was my grandfather
who abused me
(rape, Margaret, use the word rape).
Angry and relieved, deeply sad
but finally in control,
linking the pieces, I am
filled with questions.

How must I read the birthday note
penned in such style:
"December 6th, 1938.
This is for my little sweetheart Margaret
who has set back the clock
for her 'Grandpa' "?

---

*"Split at the Root," in *Nice Jewish Girls* edited by Evelyn Torton Beck (Persophone Press, 1982/ Crossing Press, 1983).

On December 6th, 1938
I was two years old.
Your hands had already begun
to cripple my vision
spiralling to find you out.
Yet the words are sweet and shine,
each a many-sided stone
cut to multiplicity of sign
and memory.

I did not set back your clock (and what
does that mean?)
You set back your clock
using your hands
your tongue your penis and my trust.
Your obsession, my availability.
Your time, safety, authority.
My gender, size, vulnerability.

I will not say again
I sat on his lap. No.
He had me on his lap.
You were not raped: he raped you.
Memory moves as it can, freedom is yours
to place the verb.
And yes, the oppressor's language
sometimes sounds beautiful,
always dies hard. Let us move on.

Easier To Match His Face

1

Easier to move
in that direction. Out, to the world.
The white-faced man, the one with three-piece suit
trailing in all my fever memories.
The one with hands.
Easier to match his face
to what they are doing to peoples, to nations.

2

His hands where they never should have been in me.
I can project them to
that man in the White House
who calls himself a contra, Joe McCarthy's ghost,
Jerry Falwell, Rambo, the District Director
of INS.

Yes he is
Guadalupe Gonzalez* in her token suit
her questions
her poor place at this table.

---

*Guadalupe Gonzalez is the Hispanic woman who was the Immigration and Naturalization Service
prosecuting attorney at my March 1986 hearing in El Paso, Texas.

3

I cannot yet evoke—what? Terror. Train my lens on
—I cannot say the word
among these others.
Cannot name it. Speak its fear in me.
A knife. A century
of death. The weight of death. Dead weight.

4

Listen. Before you die your death again in me,
I will break your hands my way, see the word
shrivel.
Reverse the power.

Guilty Of Innocence

The moon opens my palms, my hands
are full
of the distance between themselves, full
with my first power.

My schoolyard's trees are larger now, their branches
heavy, a great shade.
Memory stands up.
These trees once small as I was small.

My hands, their palms straining
against a loss of memory
(loss, no, we do not *lose*
this image of our lives.
It is taken from us. Stolen. Raped.)

Abraham Bomba speaks.*
"That night was the most horrible night
for all the people,
because of the memory of all those things
that people went through with each other
—all the joys and the happiness and the births
and the weddings and other things—
and all of a sudden, in one second, to cut through
without anything, and without any guilt of the people,
because the people weren't guilty at all.
The only guilt they had was that they were Jewish."
Abraham Bomba, survivor of Treblinka.

---

*Survival testimonies are from *Shoah*, Claude Lanzmann's oral history of the Holocaust (Pantheon, 1985).

Daily suffocation, continuous beatings, violation
of trust,
abuse and holocaust
wear the magnet thin, take power. Ours. Mine.
Hands empty at our sides, resignation
stand-in for loss.

Jewish is not guilty.
Poor is not guilty.
Black is not guilty.
Being a child, being small
is not guilty.
Woman is not guilty.
Lesbian and gay man
are not guilty.
Having a different body
is not guilty.
Having different ideas
is not guilty.

This plateau is a great and quiet place.
Cool breeze whips to wind, inflates
the world between my palms.
Take it slow, this is
all you may want to do today
and the wanting
here in your hands
is strong, your process.

Motke Zaidl and Itzhak Dugin:
"When we first opened the graves, we couldn't help it,
we all burst out sobbing. But the Germans
almost beat us to death.
We had to work at a killing pace...beaten all the time,
and with no tools. The Germans even forbade us
to use the words *corpse* or *victim*.
The dead were blocks of wood, shit,
with absolutely no importance.
Anyone who said corpse or victim
was beaten. The Germans
made us refer to the bodies as *Figuren*,
that is, as puppets, as dolls
or as *Schmates*, which means rags."
Motke Zaidl and Itzhak Dugin, survivors of Vilna.

The rape of language, the rape
of meaning.
Guilty of innocence. Innocent guilt.
Memory hibernating
when memory threatens life.
Memory coming back returns survival.

Heal with these hands, which are yours. Yourself.
Remember with these hands
which are yours.

Today I Am Older

If I tell my story
will the quail and sage take note?
Will the pink clouds of morning
pale or brighten on my eyes?

If someone asks, "Hi Meg, howya doing?"
and I reply, "I am raking through memory.
The rake's sharp teeth
furrow my belief in shadows."
Will the fixed smile crack, eyes lower
or turn away?

Who will listen to my story?
Who will open a life,
let my words sift through its sands?
Who will take a chance on me?

There is always silence,
its code and ether.
There is this race we run
clenching the starter gun between our teeth.
There is the one who says, "Here
I will give you origins, uncover eyes and shoulders
where I can,
but please don't put our name to this.
Not in the world."

What is exposure next to abuse,
my need to enter its house,
charge its back rooms,
pound and clean?

Today my body strains against the morning light,
sun-filled clouds change even as I hold them,
pieces of a great puzzle
scatter and reassemble under my feet.
Today I am older.
No hour repeats itself.

Come, together let us ready the place
with sage and crystals,
intelligent time,
generational courage.
Come, help me wake this memory from the dead.

It Will Be Necessary To Walk Through The Woods

His hands, my memories
come up in the tray. Through pale liquid
the image crowns (this metaphor
startling as I write)
the baby's head, the baby's head again and again
in this world.

First gulping contact, first breath in the place
where things are sometimes not at all.
Learn the rules, then unlearn
the rules. Practise looking away.
Refocusing your eyes
will be a lifetime concern.

Making new rules
is something we can do together.
It will be necessary
to walk through the woods.
Coaxing your energy from wrongful dust
will take a while. Let us be patient.

This is a laughing song of love
written as we go.

Coatlicue*

My hands coming up for air
survive.
The pulse opens, closes, speaks.
My necklace of skulls is scattered now.
I want to erase your nights
fearing your father's assault
upon your bed, your body.
I want to honor these women who survive. Ourselves.
Honor that part of me
standing tall beneath the rain.
When you say I haven't liked myself lately
I want to hold you
turn your face and your art
to the mirror of your life.
Make you look. And hold you without limit of time.
I also need to know that the you you do not like
is not me
crying in a dark place.
My hands come up for air, breathing
their own pulse.
The skulls of my necklace have scattered on a heavy sea.
No one should have to sleep
with a baseball bat beneath the sheets.

---

*The Aztec goddess, with necklace of bones and skulls, who ate her children. Her immense stone image can be seen in the main hall of the Museum of Anthropology and History in Mexico City.

This Is About Power

This is about power in our world.

The memory surfaces, slowly, in pieces, then larger images, longer images, but always at its own—my own—pace.

I am beginning to understand the learned need to force myself to do "the correct thing," "the proper thing," "what is expected." "Well, you know you can do it if you really want to, just try!" As if you did not want to, as if your were not trying!

That particular Protestant ethic. . . but is it only Protestant? It seems to me it is a very male way of looking at life, and our function in that. Force. Force yourself. But I can't. And moving from "I can't," to "That isn't the only way to live. . . it's not even the best way to live," to "We can create another way of life, with other values." That takes such energy, such time.

A similar analysis emerges around the idea of proof. My mother "almost believes" what I am telling her, but doubt remains. It was her father, after all. I understand why she feels the confusion of love/hate much more than I do. I've worked at this for a long time. It's my problem. It's I who have come, finally, to a place where need and ability converge. I need to do this now. I can do this now.

My mother, who surely knows she has also in some way been victimized by my grandfather's abuse, feels she is too old to do any systematized work around the issue. "It's too late for me," she says. Yet she is working . . . by supporting me. And who can say for sure? She may yet decide she needs and wants to work on her own issues. Her repeated request for proof seems transparent to me now: it's part of her work, not mine.

The male vision demands reason (in a totally transferable sense), science, proof. Intuition isn't good enough. It's such a "female" attribute. It's good enough for me.

Today Becky came out to the house. She brought the mushrooms. I had been thinking about how I would photograph them. I wanted a doll, the common kind of naked baby doll many children play with when they're small. No doll available. I wanted the mushrooms on my bed, among the sheets, close to the pillow. I got up early and changed bed linen, using a plain-colored set. Silently I note that the sheets of my childhood were simply white, and these, my only solid-colored sheets, are teal blue (my favorite color). Who would have had flowered sheets back in the thirties or early forties? Not my family.

I make a number of images of the mushrooms on my bed. Then I want them on, and next to, the scale upon which I so often and wistfully weigh myself—hoping to have lost a pound or two. A General Electric scale, symbolic of my compulsive eating. Behind the scale I prop an old teddy bear, the stand-in for the doll I had wanted. As far as I remember, I never played with a teddy bear. But a friend, who is currently confronting some serious childhood damage I imagine includes incest or some other type of strong abuse, sent me this bear. She tells me it's her oldest, most continuous and precious possession. I insist on seeing it as a loan. Another connection. So there is the image of the scale with the teddy bear and the mushrooms. I include a small picture of myself, as a child, climbing up the runged ladder of a playground slide.

With the mushrooms on the bed, I add a picture of my grandfather, the one which to me is the most frightening, a portrait of him probably taken at the time when he abused me. And I use, as well, a wonderful "adult" doll—the bearded woman Michaela, made for me by Anne Kingsbury, a Wisconsin artist and friend. Contrary to the sense of helplessness the child's doll might have evoked, Michaela symbolizes great strength and dignity. She is three and a half feet tall, made of pieces of suede leather, and stuffed. Her head is baked stoneware and her beard a series of antler points. On one side of her head is the word *free;* on the other side, *talk.* It is a powerful headpiece, an allusion to my case with the INS. The way in which Michaela holds one of her hands against her belly reminds me of the protective gesture I make with my own hands at moments in the therapy when the memories threaten to emerge.

I also have Becky place one mushroom on my night table, along with the security system panic button, telephone, asthma inhaler, and a wonderful little copy of a pre-Columbian statue—a woman with her legs spread and her round vagina laughing at the world. It was given to me by someone I love, in a moment of special warmth. I think, as I center the image, this one might be called "The Panic Button." The picture of the teddy bear and General Electric artifact could be titled "Tipping the Scale."

Now I am developing this film. Its secrets are still locked inside the canister, suspended in sixty-eight degree chemicals. This is about power, on every level.

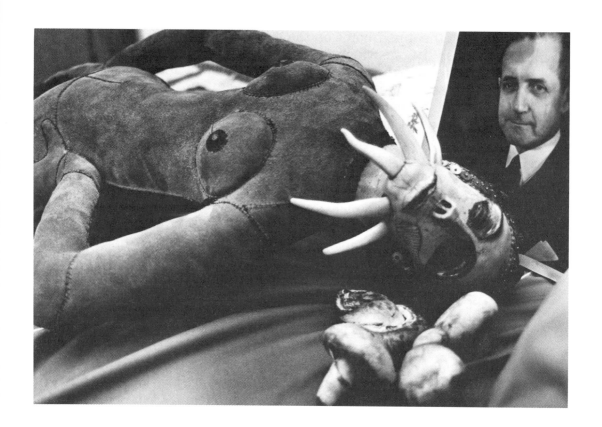

The Language Of What Really Happened

I travelled but my memory stayed behind.
I should have known
she was newborn, couldn't find her way alone.

TWA doesn't sell tickets
to underground memories
tender and vulnerable to the world.

I wanted to tell them she's female, alive, strong,
but couldn't find the words
in a language they'd understand.

And hers is the memory of language
the features of an old familiar face,
the language of criticism, the language
of what really happened
in the body, on the land.

I felt her absence
at the Vietnam War Memorial especially.
There she might have helped me connect
Quang Tri 1974 with Washington 1986.

Here I am
trying to learn from her young gift
her stubborn birthing hands
and she way off there in my mountains
waiting me home.

I shouldn't have left you alone, honey. I wouldn't have
left you alone
if I'd known.

Firebrand Books is a feminist and lesbian publishing house committed to producing quality work, in a wide variety of genres, by ethnically and racially diverse authors.

A free catalog is available on request from Firebrand Books, 141 The Commons, Ithaca, New York 14850, (607) 272-0000.